I0711431

ABORTION v. SLAVERY

THE PARALLELS BETWEEN TWO NATIONAL SINS

OLIVIA MURRAY

ABORTION v. SLAVERY

THE PARALLELS BETWEEN TWO NATIONAL SINS

OLIVIA MURRAY

TABLE OF CONTENTS

Now the days and hours and moments
Of our suff'ring seem so long;
And the toilsome wait and wond'ring
Threaten silence to our song.
Now our pain is real and pressing
Where our faith is thin and weak,
But our hope is set on Jesus;
And we cling to him, our strength.
Oh eternal weight of glory!
Oh inheritance divine!
We will see our Lord redeeming
Every past and future time.
All our pains will be transfigured,
Like the scars of Christ our Lord.
We will see the weight of glory,
And our broken years restored.
For behold! I tell a myst'ry:
At the trumpet sound we'll wake
"Death is swallowed up in vict'ry!"
When we meet our King of Grace
Every year we thought was wasted
Every night we cried "How long?"
All will be a passing moment
In our Savior's vict'ry song.

We will see our wounded Savior.
We'll behold him face to face;
And we'll hear our anguished stories
Sung as vict'ry songs of grace.

-Wendell Kimbrough

INTRODUCTION

I would be remiss should I understate how heavily my relationship with Jesus Christ influenced this booklet. My interest in Christian apologetics became the catalyst for this work and I hope these words and images will inspire the reader to further consider the arguments presented.

American journalist Sydney Harris once wrote, "History repeats itself, but in such cunning disguise that we never detect the resemblance until the damage is done."

Slavery as practiced in the British colonies and post-independence is rightfully considered one of the darkest moments in American history. The barbarism and replete derision suffered by Americans in chains is almost entirely synonymous with the final experience of those in the womb who are slated for execution. Employed by both proponents of abortion and slavery are the same tactics and reasoning in an effort to justify the unjustifiable.

With General Robert E. Lee's surrender at Appomattox in April 1865, the Civil War ended and slavery was legally an institution of the past. The wake of destruction made manifest by brutal and forced servitude is monumental. Millions oppressed under the yoke of subjugation, immeasurable lives lost to the violence of battle or the maltreatment of the plantations, shattered families broken by cruel indifference, lynching mobs intent on murder instead of justice, and fractured race relations existing still today.

Just as we endure the fallout from the national sin of slavery, I fear the aftermath from the carnage of abortion will be far more consequential. It is in this spirit I write, as I seek to expound upon the literary foundation of the anti-abortion movement.

I hope to encourage and equip others to fight, not against our fellow man, but against insidious schemes and deceptions. Nothing done for the kingdom of God is done in vain, and we assuredly know the Lord of all creation is on the side of those who seek to protect the most vulnerable and defenseless among us. God bless.

1
DEHUMANIZE THE CONDEMNED POPULATION
—
"Not a Person"

Efforts to subject particular populations to a category of "sub-human" are, and have long been, a standard operating procedure of psychological warfare and manipulation. The Merriam-Webster dictionary defines "dehumanize" as: "to address or portray [someone] in a way that obscures or demeans that person's humanity or individuality."[1] In order to legitimize their attacks, both proponents of slavery and abortion adopted the recognized euphemism, "not a person." To influence the public and culturally reinforce this notion, victimizers primarily utilize(d) a misleading lexicon and inaccurate depictions of the marginalized populaces. The language used by defenders of slavery and abortion is, and was, specifically designed to portray animalistic imagery, thereby making it easier to paint the respective group as insentient; unable to feel or understand things.

SLAVERY

→ "apes, monkeys"
These racist slurs, caricatures, and "scientific" illustrations or "evidence" depicted blacks as simian in their features and characteristics.

This image appeared in a well-known scientific text of the 1800s. Intended to strengthen the argument that blacks were evolutionarily closer to apes.

→ "coon"/ "nigger"
A racial slur as well as a caricature. The name itself is abbreviated from "raccoon," and portrayed blacks as uncivilized and possessing only the most rudimentary cognitive abilities.[2]

Demeans blacks by portraying them as foolish appropriators of European fashion. The drawing suggests that despite their polished attire, they can never attain societal and cultural equality.

ABORTION

→ "clump of cells"

Accurate; however, a human being at every stage of development is, simply put, a "clump of cells." That doesn't determine humanity. For example, a toddler is not less human or deserving of life than a teenager because the toddler is made up of less cells.

→ "parasite"

Wildly inaccurate; a parasite *by definition* is a different species than the host and cannot include symbiosis.

A biological example of how erroneous the term "parasite" is, can be seen through the scientific phenomenon, "fetal cell microchimerism." This is when stem cells from a child in the womb migrate into the mother without rejection (despite differences in DNA). This may occur during pregnancy, or decades after the birth of the child.[3] A 2015 study in the peer-reviewed medical journal, *Circulation Research*, concluded: "fetal maternal stem cell transfer appears to be a critical mechanism in the maternal response to cardiac injury."[4]

In simpler terms: if a mother is experiencing heart injury or failure, stem cells from the unborn child will be sent to repair the damaged tissue.

An image that sparked outcry in 2019 from a pro-choice rally in which three women brandished a sign referring to humans as "parasites."

→ "fertilized egg"
Accurate; yet "zygote" is the more common biological term for the newly created human being at the moment of conception.

→ "product of conception"
Accurate; this is intended to remove the idea they are referring to a unique and living human being.

→ "fetus"
Accurate; this is the scientific and medical reference to the child in the womb any time after the 8th week (gestational age).[5]

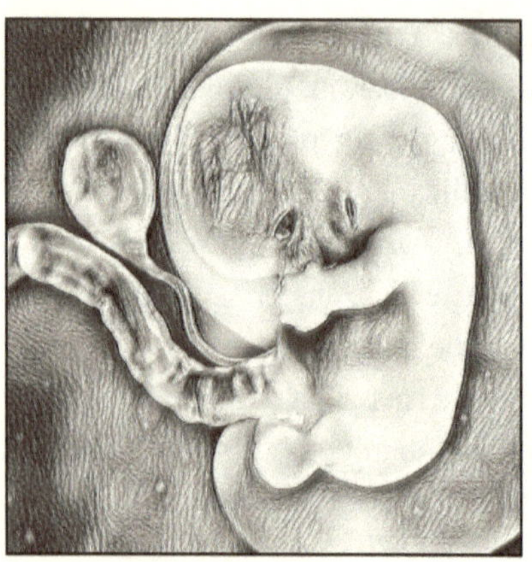

A sketch of a fetus at 6 weeks
(8 weeks gestational age).

The objective of dehumanizing certain groups of people is ultimately to demean them to a status where they don't qualify for personhood at all. Liberty and equality for blacks in America suffered a major hindrance in 1857 when the Supreme Court adjudicated on the landmark case, *Dred Scott v. Sandford*,* or more commonly known as the "Dred Scott Decision." Scott was a slave, who, at several times, accompanied his master to territories where slavery was illegal. He claimed these voyages to free states rendered him emancipated, prompting him to sue for his freedom. The case eventually landed before the Supreme Court, and in a 7-2 split, the Court determined Scott was "not a person."[6] Chief Justice Roger B. Taney wrote in the majority opinion:

> The question before us is whether the class of persons described in the plea in abatement compose a portion of this people, and are constituent members of this sovereignty? We think they are not, and that they are not included, and were not intended to be included, under the word "citizens" in the Constitution, and can therefore claim none of the rights and privileges which that instrument provides for and secures to citizens of the United States.[7]

Synonymous with the majority opinion in the Dred Scott decision is the conclusion arrived to by the Supreme Court concerning *Roe v. Wade*. Under the pseudonym of "Jane Roe," Norma McCorvey of Texas challenged the state's legislation on abortion, claiming the law robbed her of her right to privacy and her liberty, citing the First, Fourth, Fifth, Ninth and Fourteenth Amendments.[8] The outcome of this case established legal precedent, with the Supreme Court determining that women had the right to

---

* John Sanford's last name was incorrectly spelled "Sandford" in court documents.

abortion before viability* without undue interference from the government. After the child was viable, the state had the authority to restrict or prohibit abortion procedures *and* the state has a well-founded interest in protecting the woman's health and the life of the unborn.(9) Not surprisingly, the arguments made in the majority opinion relied entirely on the ascertainment that the unborn was "not a person."(10) Coincidentally, the court mirrored the 7-2 split of *Scott v. Sandford*, with Associate Justice Harry Blackmun penning the majority opinion. In it he wrote, "the Constitution does not define *person*" and that if it were to do so, "the appellant's case, of course, collapses, for the fetus' right to life would then be guaranteed specifically by the [Fourteenth] Amendment."

Undeniably, legal and constitutional scholars on both sides agree that our supreme governing document, the Constitution, does in fact refer to those held in bondage. Not only does the Constitution refer to slaves, but it refers to slaves as "persons;" Article 1, Section 2, Clause 3, reads "all other persons" while delineating representation and taxes.(11)

In 1857, despite the clear and objective truth that slaves were both ethically AND legally people, the Court failed to render justice and morality. This misapplication of the law was echoed 116 years later in 1973, when the Court once again determined a specific class of people was not entitled to our inalienable rights protected by the Constitution. Although in this case the Constitution doesn't explicitly designate the unborn as people, the Fifth Amendment enumerates that no one shall "be deprived of life, liberty, or property, without due process

---

*At the time *Roe v. Wade* was decided in 1973, viability was considered as early as 24 weeks, or the beginning of the second trimester.

of law."(12) The absence of an explicit annotation defining the unborn as beings with inherent rights provided a way for Justice Blackmun to entertain lexical and irrational technicalities, thus creating a right to abortion that is empirically missing. Blackmun argued that the question of when life began was uncertain, writing:

> When those trained in the respective disciplines of medicine, philosophy, and theology are unable to arrive at any consensus, the judiciary, at this point in the development of man's knowledge, is not in a position to speculate as to the answer.

Since 1973, the fields of medicine and science have experienced rapid and profound growth in terms of knowledge and technology. Dr. Marjorie England, a distinguished member of the University of Leicester Medical School, wrote extensively about life beginning at conception. In her groundbreaking and most recognized volume, England wrote:

> Development of the embryo begins at Stage 1 when a sperm fertilizes an oocyte and together they form a zygote.(13)

Countless embryology medical texts all concur, concluding a new human life begins at the moment of conception. Excerpts from some of the medical community's most respected works are listed here:

> Human development begins after the union of male and female gametes or germ cells during process known as *fertilization* (conception).

> Fertilization is a sequence of events that begins with the contact of a *sperm* (spermatozoon) with a

secondary oocyte (ovum) and ends with the fusion of their *pronuclei* (the haploid nuclei of the sperm and ovum) and the mingling of their chromosomes to form a new cell. The fertilized ovum, known as a *zygote*, is a large diploid cell that is the beginning, or *primordium of a human being*.(14)

And:

The development of a human being begins with fertilization, a process by which two highly specialized cells, the *spermatozoon* from the male and the *oocyte* from the female, unite to give rise to a new organism, the *zygote*.(15)

Due to developments within the "respective disciplines" referenced by Justice Blackmun, it appears the dutiful option now is to not only reverse *Roe v. Wade*, but outlaw abortion in its entirety. Just as there are no moral or legal justifications to quell a group of people into forced servitude, there are also no grounds to excuse or legalize abortion in any capacity.

The Supreme Court, circa 1973.

Consider the irony of pro-abortion advocates when they pontificate: "no uterus, no opinion" — yet the only reason they have a legal right to kill their children is due to the opinions of seven men.

My Property, My Choice — My Body, My Choice

One of the most notable and obvious parallels of dehumanizing terminology is that of the victim being referred to as *property*. As those exploited by slavery did not amount to personhood, it is no surprise they were referred to as "property," bought and sold like "livestock," and subjected to "breeding programs." Complete ownership of a fellow human being entitled a "master" to treat their property however they chose, even if that included abuse, torture, or death. Extracted from a personal letter, the following excerpt details particular wickedness suffered by a slave at the hands of an overseer:

> One Gibbs, overseer for Mrs. P., mounted on horseback, took him [the slave] from confinement, compelled him to run back to Elkton, a distance of fifteen miles, whipping him all the way. When he reached home, the negro exhausted and worn out, exclaimed 'you have broke my heart,' i.e. you have killed me. For this, Gibbs flew into a violent passion, tied the negro to a stake, and, in the language of a witness, *'cut his back to mince-meat.'* But the fiend was not satisfied with this. He burnt his legs to a blister, with hot embers, and then chained him *naked*, in the open air, weary with running, weak from the loss of blood, and smarting from his burns.

The incident above led to the death of the victim the following morning, and unsurprisingly, Gibbs "escaped without even *the shadow* of a trial."(16) This negro man was property under the law, entitling Gibbs to do whatever he pleased without any legal ramifications.

Identically, today there is a rallying cry so oft repeated it's mind-numbing: "my body, my choice." This can be interpreted in two different ways; the life inside the mother is not a separate life but rather an extension of the mother, OR the child in the womb is a child, but because of its location the child belongs to the mother and is her property, and she can therefore do as she wishes. In a context or setting where abortion is contested, supporters of the practice appear anesthetized to analytical thinking. The slogan is rabidly screamed in order to silence, or monotonously echoed to shut down any thought-provoking or critical opposition. It appears the painful lack of awareness is widespread, leading to a fallacious position; abortion proponents are begging the claim. Those spouting off "my body, my choice" are operating on the false premise that abortion only involves the woman, ignoring science and logic. Medically and scientifically, the moment of conception is when the DNA of the new human being is determined, and is entirely unique to that of the mother's. If those fighting for the "right to choose" were correct, and the child's body was the mother's body, then at conception, she would have two unique sets of DNA; however, this is impossible, and therefore they are conclusively wrong.

Recognition of man does not determine humanity; both the unnamed negro and the unborn child received an endowment of sacred value at the moment of their creation. Their right to life and safety is not contingent on whether their fellow man believes they deserve such things — it is contingent upon reality. Human beings cannot morally be made property, and when the law allows for such a colossal lapse in justice, the fight for abolition of such a grievance becomes duty.

2
INVOKE COMPASSION AND SYMPATHY

—

Suggest the Evil is Best for the Victim

This may be the most insidious and deceptive tactic of all. The individual or group advocating for slavery or abortion claims the moral high ground, attempting to manipulate by appealing to a sense of empathy and duty to support the "utilitarian" evil, alleging the institution for which they promote is actually what is best for the respective population. Whether the respective party intentionally aims to subjugate or not, this is a sadistic exploitation of both the general public as well as the oppressed group. Most regretfully, the advocates of both slavery and abortion refer(red) to the Bible as an authoritative source to validate their position.

SLAVERY

An 1855 book titled *Slavery, Indispensable to the Civilization of Africa* by Samuel McKenney expounds upon the notion that slavery is a compassionate and moral business. Relying on the Christian responsibility to the Great Commandment and the Great Commission, McKenney argues that the only conceivable way to bring progress and preservation to the continent of Africa is through slavery. Citing the inhospitable conditions abroad, he postulates that enlightenment must happen in America. According to McKenney, in order for this to take place, "the captivity of some portion of her children [Africans];" is necessary, and "they must be sold to a foreign land and become the property of strangers." He expresses his frustration with those who denounce slavery alleging they have a "dim and distorted" view:

> It is not unfrequent that slavery is denounced by very good people as a sin in the sight of heaven, - a wickedness so shocking as to be without excuse of palliation. And they point to the orderly upright conduct of many slaves… as proof of the heinousness of an institution which keeps such people in bondage… The facts which are thus produced as an argument against the morality and humanity of slavery, are the very facts which go to establish both! I ask, where these upright and excellent characters amongst the African race in our country came from? Do they not owe their existence to slavery? These are the very fruits which the African enjoys as a consequence of his bondage.(1)

At best, McKenney's motives were altruistic, although misplaced. Regardless of whether McKenney sought benevolence for the African race or not, objectively speaking, the institution of slavery was a heavy grievance against his fellow man. This is analogous with those who advocate for abortion today (again, assuming the best), that despite their compassion for the mother and her unborn, taking the life of the child is murder and therefore causes irreparable harm to the mother. This may be summed up with the commonly known phrase, "The road to Hell is paved with good intentions."

ABORTION

As the nation's largest provider of abortion, the Planned Parenthood Federation of America, Inc. maintains a *Clergy Advocacy Board* (CAB), composed of clergy and spiritual leaders from a variety of faiths and denominations across the country. The CAB "leads a national effort to increase public awareness of the theological and moral basis for advocating reproductive health and justice."[2] On top of pastoral or ministerial duties, these men and women pen essays, op-eds, and articles featured in publications such as *The New York Times* and *The Huffington Post*.

Pro-abortion voices from across the country consistently call on scripture to bolster their agenda; often prefacing their pitch with "the war on women." A member of CAB and an invitee to the White House by President Barack Obama's Interfaith Education Initiative, Reverend Jes Kast holds a theological view in which a Holy God approves of abortion. In a 2019 interview with *The Atlantic,* Rev. Kast discussed her doctrine:

> Interviewer: So, just to be clear, what do you think is the Christian theological argument for abortion?

> Rev. Kast: When people talk about "Our body is a temple of God, and holy," I see that as *I* have the right to choices over my body, and the freedom to make the decisions that are right for me.

Apart from the fact an ordained minister was unable to correctly cite the verse she attempted to reference, this is a patently illogical perspective. She completely ignores the fact that abortion also involves the body of the child. This belief could be used by a pedophile to justify pedophilia, or a rapist to justify a rape. After all, they would simply be exercising their personal right to "choice" and "freedom" albeit at the expense of someone else. Yet she goes on:

> Rev. Kast: (referencing John 10:10, although she only could pinpoint "Gospel of John") God's plan for our lives is to actually have a meaningful life with loving contentment and satisfaction.
>
> Because of that—because I value life, and I believe Jesus values life—I value the choices that give us the type of life that we need.(3)

Again, Kast is painfully blind to her own sinful foolishness. By her logic, any person could justify any wrong or wicked action because they deem it necessary to give them "the type of life" that they need. She concludes by stating, "even God doesn't have the final say over how we make the choices that are best for us." If those who claim to be a faithful servant to the Lord do not believe one of the most basic tenets of Christianity (His ultimate sovereignty), then they are undeniably false prophets.

***

According to the *Pew Research Center*, the following major religious groups officially endorse abortion rights with few or no restrictions: United Church of Christ, Unitarian Universalist, Reform Judaism, Presbyterian Church (U.S.A.), and Conservative Judaism.(4)

An extremely familiar argument, and a *slippery slope* and *either/or fallacy*, is the idea that the child is undesired, and therefore will grow up in an abusive home, or unwanted in foster care. Advocates paint a devastating picture of innocent children growing up in a world without love, suggesting the most benevolent action is to instead slaughter the child before birth. Margaret Sanger, the founder of the American Birth Control League (the predecessor to Planned Parenthood), often opined, "the most merciful thing that a large family does to one of its infant members is to kill it."[5]

Of course, the landscape portrayed by advocates of abortion in this instance is desolate. Those who fight for life are profoundly saddened by the reality that some children are subject to abuse or abandonment. However, this assertion is fallacious in several aspects. To the address of each:

- slippery slope:
Conclusion founded on the assumption that if A happens, eventually, through a negligible sequence of events, then Z will also happen. In order to prevent Z, then we must also prevent A.

Example: "If we don't allow abortion, then children will grow up unwanted and unloved." This ignores all the other variables and factors that could reasonably lead to a positive outcome for children conceived in unplanned pregnancies.

- either/or:
Oversimplification of the argument, minimizing it to only two sides.

Example: "Either allow abortion, or children will be abused and abandoned." Clearly, this is ridiculous, as children rescued from abortion have grown up in loving homes, and planned children have experienced abuse and neglect.

***

The authority of the Bible assigns extreme weight and credibility to its words, yet any endeavor to ascribe morality to a clear injustice is fraudulent and underhanded. Abortion advocates proceed to build upon the biblical argument, claiming the noble and caring response to unintended pregnancies is a preemptive and willful murder of the child.

3

A PETITION TO REASON & LOGIC

—

"Necessary for Survival"

Any attempt to condone injustice by claiming it is the rational thing to do is ludicrous. This defense was prominent during the era of slavery in America, and is frequently relied on now by supporters of abortion. One argument in particular is identical, while others are not. Either way, proponents of both institutions deemed the integrity of the individual social fixture was the utilitarian option for survival. Whether it's slavery or abortion, the defender's strategy was/is to argue that if abolition occurred, it would reap more destruction and suffering than maintaining the institution itself.

SLAVERY

Although objectively false, a primary source document details the sentiment held by many proponents of slavery; it was fundamental for economic strength and stability. From a London newspaper published in 1789, the writer propagated the notion that the stability of the entire British empire depended upon slavery. Addressed to abolitionists, referred to as "the supporters of that alarming measure," the article read, "without the trade your ill-judged zeal wants to put an end to," there would be no cultivation of lands or manufacturing. He implored the readers to consider a judicious and impartial analysis of what was at stake:

Are you prepared with a fund to make up a compensation to the planters, merchants, and thousands of annuitants, whose daily bread depends on the produce of this beneficial commerce with the West India Islands?

And:

If you give up your trade, what must become of your navy, the bulwark of England? - remember that every mariner you lose for want of employment, goes into the scale of rival nations, who have, at this moment, agents, fomenting this madness that has spread itself amongst the multitude.(1)

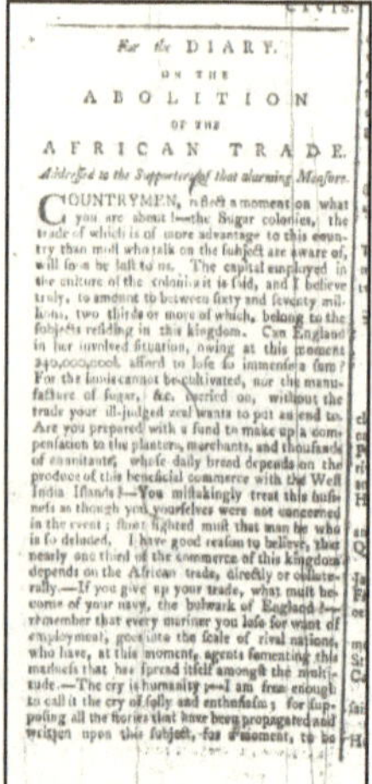

Image from the original newspaper article from the late 1700s.

His petition to the "zealots" against slavery attempted to appeal to their acumen, adducing the presumed ill-fated bankruptcy of those dependent on slave labor as well as the British empire itself. This manipulation and position is now common among those arguing in favor of abortion. They too solicit their audience to consider the greater affects upon humanity if unborn babies receive life in lieu of death.

<u>ABORTION</u>

Arguments heard today oftentimes include the idea that abortion is indispensable due to economic reasons. This argument suggests that abortion is necessary and cannot be outlawed, otherwise there will be a surge of children put into foster care, creating a massive burden on the state and therefore the taxpayers. This is yet another slippery slope fallacy; if abortion were outlawed, it does not guarantee there would be a massive uptick of children in the foster care system (irrelevant anyways; an overburdened foster care system does not legitimize murdering the innocent). People might choose to lead more responsible sex lives or, in the event of an unintended pregnancy, they might opt to parent instead of face legal consequences.

The list of politicians, world leaders, and organizations that promote abortion as a tool to curb population growth to mitigate the "climate crisis" goes on ad nauseam. Without population control, they anticipate such severe and irreversible environmental degradation that they believe abortion is absolutely crucial. There are seemingly infinite examples, with the most recognizable highlighted below, in order to illustrate how radical and nefarious this idea is:

- <u>The *WHO (World Health Organization), the United Nations,* and The World Bank</u>
  For "International Safe Abortion Day 2020," the Human Reproduction Programme (cosponsored by the UNDP/UNFPA/UNICEF/WHO/World Bank, with International Planned Parenthood Federation [IPPF] as a member of the governing body) announced major collaborations with international groups to promote abortion across

the globe.(2) The five parent groups as well as IPPF espouse radical climate change agendas, and cite "access to reproductive health" as a means to the end of "sustainability." In an adopted document outlining a "reproductive health strategy," the *WHO* committed to accountability on "progress towards reproductive and sexual health as part of achieving the Millennium Development Goals (MDGs)."(3) According to the *WHO*, the MDGs have been superseded by the "Sustainable Development Goals," or SDGs. Despite the benevolent tone of the list, to accomplish the enumerated objectives like "take urgent action to combat climate change and its impacts," expanding access to and increasing the number of abortions is an indispensable step.(4)

- *The Population Council*
Headquartered in New York City, the mission of this nonprofit is "to improve the well-being and reproductive health of current and future generations around the world and to help achieve a humane, equitable, and sustainable balance between people and resources."(5) This organization explicitly references the SDGs of the *United Nations* and affirms it is in this context they operate, and with whom they align.

- *Greenpeace*
An organization whose apparently sole focus is environmental conservation, rampantly endorses the abortion agenda. A 2019 article written by staff member Alice Newberry underscores the

perspective that abortion is wholly necessary for climate management. She writes, "access to abortion and reproductive healthcare is fundamentally tied to environmental justice," and "by eliminating abortion access we remove a critical piece of health care necessary for the well-being of people and the planet."[6]

- _Black Lives Matter_ and
  The Movement for Black Lives
  With goals of sweeping systemic and cultural change, these organizations have experienced a meteoric rise. One of the core "policy platforms" of _Movement for Black Lives_ is "End the War on Black People," but more specifically, "End the War on Black Health and Black Disabled People." In it, they make a list of "demands," and, not surprisingly, "the full range of reproductive health care services, comprehensive sex education, contraception, and **abortion**" (emphasis added) is highlighted.[7]

Particularly in the wake of the 2020 riots, the hypocrisy of an organization that frequently opted for violence yet contained the word "life" in its name, became obvious to many — aside from promoting genocide of the black community.

- *World Population Balance*
  and *One Planet, One Child*
  World Population Balance (WPB) aims to bring attention to the dangers of "overpopulation" in order to sustain a smaller global population by lowering birth rates, and is the creator of the *One Planet, One Child* marketing campaign.[8] As one might easily deduce, this faction of WPB prioritizes abortion through affiliations and advertisements. Their website provides several options to "support family planning around the world;" one to *Pathfinder International* and the other to *United Nations Population Fund (UNFPA),* both of which wholly promote abortion. Slogans like *"Traffic Congestion Begins at Conception"* and *"Overpopulation: Bleak Job Prospects, Traffic Congestion, Sky-High Rent, Pandemics,"* are blatant fear-mongering attempts to appeal to a member of the general public's logical sense of self and familial preservation.[9]

- *Zhao Beige, former vice minister of China's National Population and Family Planning Commission*
  From 1980-2016, the Chinese Communist Party (CCP) embraced a "one-child policy." This resulted in, among other things, state violence by means of forced abortions. Despite the apparent lack of acknowledgement from the CCP itself, multiple media outlets, journalists, Chinese citizens, and human rights groups have testified to the veracity of this extreme measure. At a

2009 *United Nations* climate change conference, Zhao Beige touted China's population program, saying "[China] has made a great historic contribution to the well-being of society." She made the claim that with 400 million fewer births, CO_2 emissions decreased by 18 million tons per year. Although she stated "I'm not saying that what we have done is 100 percent right," she believed they were going in the right direction as "1.3 billion people had benefited." [10]

Though both platforms gain(ed) support for economic reasons, those pushing for abortion today tout it as not only a necessary evil, but actively encourage further occurrences of the practice. Despite abortion being the most commonly performed medical procedure in the United States, maintaining the status quo is not sufficient. As shown above, global organizations intend to push abortion across the world in order to ensure *their* ideal population size.

4

PORTRAYING ABORTION AS A LOSING BATTLE

—

You Cannot Legislate Morality

As is standard for anyone advocating for injustice to be accepted or enshrined into law, the accompanying arguments are often nonsensical. Just because people *WILL* commit wicked acts does not mean a society ought to tolerate or legally allow for them. Seemingly, this notion would be easily discerned by any member of a civilized society, but was/is somehow arduously grasped (if at all) by supporters of slavery and abortion.

SLAVERY

Temple Luttrell, a member of the British aristocracy made an impassioned speech to Parliament in 1777. He argued, in the event of abolition and Britain's involvement in the commercial slave trade ceased, other nations would fill the void and the slave trade would continue. For Luttrell, Britain's departure would not quell the international commerce of slave labor desired by abolitionists; they would simply be eclipsed by other monarchs in their colonial development and the conditions of the slaves in bondage would decline.[1]

Though Luttrell seemingly predicted a likely outcome, it is inconsequential to the morality (rather, immorality) of slavery.

ABORTION

Proponents of abortion often state the obvious; "women are still going to get abortions." The pro-life/anti-abortion crowd acknowledges that reality - just as people are still going to commit murder, rape, theft, etc. Whether there exists a penal code or not, the certainty of human sin is a guarantee. However, as a civil society, morality is demanded and necessary to properly function. The law does not stop ALL criminal behavior, but it absolutely influences the extent to which it occurs. When a jurisdiction (local or national) chooses to decriminalize certain actions, a sharp rise in the respective conduct ensues. Examples of this are easily found, but the historical evidence of abortion rates is apropos. According to the Guttmacher Institute, from the 1973 legalization until around 1981-1982, abortion rates skyrocketed.[2]

In order to maintain the legality of such evils, proponents of slavery and abortion depend(ed) on tactics of manipulation to bolster their position. Since logic and reason are not in favor of either immorality, the contentions of their supporters openly display their shaky ground. A keynote identifier of the pro-abortion position is the naïve inclination to claims that are emotional and ignorant. Notwithstanding the difficulty experienced in reining in flimsy arguments, defenders of life must dutifully engage and equip themselves for combat against such incoherent thoughts.

CONCLUSION

Although over one hundred years stands between the abolition of slavery and the legalization of abortion, the justifications for each bear a heavy resemblance. The purpose of this work is to provide a brief overview of this niche argument, while furnishing some of the subtleties. I strived to equip the reader with logic and facts to better defend the anti-abortion position. To undo the harm already done is impossible. However, we've been given the opportunity to fight for the defenseless, and by the grace of the Lord, we may yet conquer the current culture of death.

As we are instructed in Paul's epistle to the church in Colossae, "whatsoever ye do in word or deed, do all in the name of the Lord Jesus." God bless you all.

GRATITUDE

First and foremost, I am deeply thankful to my Lord and Savior for His blessing and direction on this work. To Him goes all the glory.

I am sincerely grateful to several people for their support with this project, but above all I want to recognize one of my closest friends, Michael Jolls. Not only is Michael responsible for so much directly concerning the production and publishing of this booklet, but he is one of my greatest supporters and allies. He has been consistent and encouraging, and I am truly thankful for his kindness and favor. The inspiration to address this topic is due to Father Richard Simon. He is a bold voice for the unborn, and for that I am truly appreciative. I would like to thank my mother and grandmother, who are always available to take my calls and offer constructive affirmations and criticisms. Next, I am incredibly thankful for Craig Magruder of Kentucky. Craig has been a rock and a father to me, always inclusive and loving, supporting me as if I was his own. His constancy and positive reinforcement in my life have truly been a gift. I would like to express sincere thanks to my dear friends Joe and Ann Scheidler of Chicago, and Dr. Monica Miller of Michigan. They possess qualities of boldness and stamina that are deeply admired while their brilliance and servant leadership is unrivaled. They have lived lives of absolute sacrifice, and I hope to follow their example. Also deserving of great regard is Dan Jolls, who donated his expertise and considerable time to professionally edit this work. Lastly, without the love and support of Steve and Jean Lillmars of Pennsylvania, this endeavor would be nonexistent. I am deeply indebted to their Christ-like love and gratefulness, as they have set an example to love as Jesus did.

To all those who fight for the unborn and their families, I extend my heartfelt thankfulness. God bless you all.

ENDNOTES

Chapter 1 – Dehumanize the Condemned Population

1. "Dehumanize." *The Merriam-Webster.Com Dictionary*, www.merriam-webster.com/dictionary/dehumanize. Accessed 13 Nov. 2020.
2. Pilgrim, David. "The Coon Caricature." *Jim Crow Museum of Racist Memorabilia*, Ferris State University, Oct. 2000, www.ferris.edu/HTMLS/news/jimcrow/coon/homepage.htm.
3. Bianchi, D. W., et al. "Male Fetal Progenitor Cells Persist in Maternal Blood for as Long as 27 Years Postpartum." *Proceedings of the National Academy of Sciences*, vol. 93, no. 2, 1996, pp. 705–08, doi:10.1073/pnas.93.2.705.
4. Kara, Rina J., et al. "Fetal Cells Traffic to Injured Maternal Myocardium and Undergo Cardiac Differentiation." *Circulation Research*, vol. 110, no. 1, 2012, pp. 82–93, doi:10.1161/circresaha.111.249037.
5. "Fetal Development: Month-By-Month Stages of Pregnancy." *Cleveland Clinic*, my.clevelandclinic.org/health/articles/7247-fetal-development-stages-of-growth. Accessed 13 Nov. 2020.
6. "Dred Scott v. Sandford." *Oyez*, www.oyez.org/cases/1850-1900/60us393. Accessed 16 Nov. 2020.
7. United States Supreme Court, et al. The Dred Scott decision: opinion of Chief Justice Taney. New York: Van Evrie, Horton & Co., 1860, 1860. Pdf. Retrieved from the Library of Congress, <www.loc.gov/item/17001543/>.
8. "Jane ROE, et al., Appellants, v. Henry WADE." *LII / Legal Information Institute*, www.law.cornell.edu/supremecourt/text/410/113. Accessed 10 Nov. 2020.
9. Ibid. (8).
10. Ibid. (8).
11. U.S. Constitution. Article 1, Section 2.
12. U.S. Constitution, Amendment V.
13. England, Marjorie A. Life Before Birth. 2nd ed. England: Mosby-Wolfe, 1996, p. 31.
14. Herbst, Marlene, et al. Essentials of Human Embryology. United Kingdom, B.C. Decker, 1988.
15. Langman, Jan. Medical Embryology. 3rd ed. Baltimore: Williams and Wilkins, 1975, p. 3
16. American Slavery as it is: Testimony of a Thousand Witnesses. Italy, American Anti-Slavery Society, 1839, p. 70.

Chapter 2 – Invoke Compassion and Sympathy

1. McKenney, Samuel. Slavery Indispensable to the Civilization of Africa. Baltimore: Printed by John D. Toy, 1855.
2. "Restrictions on Safe, Legal Abortion." *Planned Parenthood*, Aug. 2014, www.plannedparenthood.org/about-us/our-leadership/clergy-advocacy-board/our-values/restrictions-safe-legal-abortion.

3.   Green, Emma. "Why Some Progressive Christians Support Abortion Rights." *The Atlantic*, 29 May 2019, www.theatlantic.com/politics/archive/2019/05/progressive-christians-abortion-jes-kast/590293.

4.   Masci, David. "Where major religious groups stand on abortion." *Pew Research Center*, 21 June 2016, https://www.pewresearch.org/fact-tank/2016/06/21/where-major-religious-groups-stand-on-abortion/. Accessed 10 Nov. 2020.

5.   Katz, Esther. "The Editor as Public Authority: Interpreting Margaret Sanger." *The Public Historian*, vol. 17, no. 1, 1995. pp. 41-50. *JSTOR*, www.jstor.org/stable/3378350. Accessed 23 Nov. 2020.

Chapter 3 – A Petition to Reason and Logic

1.   "On the Abolition of the African Trade." *The Diary* or *Woodfall's Register* [London, England], 16 Apr. 1789, www.bl.uk/learning/histcitizen/campaignforabolition/sources/proslavery/proslaveryarticle/proslaveryarticle.html.

2.   "International Safe Abortion Day." *World Health Organization*, 28 Sept. 2020, www.who.int/news/item/28-09-2020-international-safe-abortion-day.

3.   *Reproductive Health Strategy To Accelerate Progress Towards The Attainment Of International Development Goals And Targets.* 1st ed. [ebook] Geneva: World Health Organization, p. 31. Available at: <https://apps.who.int/iris/bitstream/handle/10665/68754/WHO_RHR_04.8.pdf?sequence=1> [Accessed 20 Nov. 2020].

4.   "Sustainable Development Goals (SDGs)." *World Health Organization*, apps.who.int/iris/bitstream/handle/10665/68754/WHO_RHR_04.8.pdf?sequence=1. Accessed 20 Nov. 2020.

5.   "Strategic Priorities: Mission." *Population Council*, www.popcouncil.org/about/strategic-priorities. Accessed 20 Nov. 2020.

6.   Newberry, Alice. "Why We Can't Have Environmental Justice without Reproductive Justice." *Greenpeace USA*, 27 Sept. 2019, www.greenpeace.org/usa/envirojusticexreprojustice.

7.   "END THE WAR ON BLACK HEALTH AND BLACK DISABLED PEOPLE." *Movement 4 Black Lives*, m4bl.org/policy-platforms/end-the-war-black-health. Accessed 20 Nov. 2020.

8.   "Vision and Mission." World Population Balance, www.worldpopulationbalance.org/wpb_mission_statement. Accessed 5 Nov. 2020.

9.   "Home Page." *One Planet, One Child*, oneplanetonechild.org. Accessed 20 Nov. 2020.

10.   Xing, Li. "Population Control Called Key to Deal." *China Daily,* 2009, www.chinadaily.com.cn/china/2009-12/10/content_9151129.htm.

Chapter 4 – Portraying Abortion as a Losing Battle

1.   Luttrell, Temple. "If We Don't Trade, Others Will." 23 May, 1777. *The Abolition Project.* http://gallery.nen.gov.uk/audio78790-abolition.html.

2.   "Induced Abortion in the United States." *Guttmacher Institute*, 8 May 2020, www.guttmacher.org/fact-sheet/induced-abortion-united-states#.

LIST OF PHOTOGRAPHS

14 – *The Evolution of Man*, 1874 edition. Public Domain – Old.

14 – Ferris State University. The Jim Crow Museum of Racist Memorabilia. Public Domain – Old.

15 – From a pro-abortion rally in Huntsville, Alabama, May 2019. The faces have been blurred. Original photographer unknown.

16 – Sketch of an embryo. Image donated by private artist.

20 – Supreme Court of the United States. June 1972. Public Domain.

32 – Public Domain – Old.

35 – Sketch of a *Black Lives Matter* protest. Image donated by private artist.

INDEX

Discover the incredible life of a German immigrant whose legacy embodies the American dream!

About the Author

Olivia Murray has a BA in History from the University of Arizona. In 2019, she founded *Life for Unborn Children*, a 501(c)(3) non-profit, focusing on an apologetics approach towards anti-abortion education and supporting young mothers in unplanned pregnancies. She is a mother to two boys. Very passionate about modern politics and a staunch supporter of the Second Amendment, Olivia maintains involvement in local community efforts to promote constitutional freedoms.

www.ingramcontent.com/pod-product-compliance
Lightning Source LLC
Chambersburg PA
CBHW051357250726
48656CB00006B/2130